M. O. T. H.

M.O.T.H

Matters of the Heart
"A Book of Poetry"

Melissa Monék

authorHOUSE®

AuthorHouse™ LLC
1663 Liberty Drive
Bloomington, IN 47403
www.authorhouse.com
Phone: 1-800-839-8640

Published by AuthorHouse   06/16/2014

ISBN: 978-1-4969-1931-1 (sc)
ISBN: 978-1-4969-1930-4 (e)

This book is dedicated to everyone who believes in love, ever felt love, and knows what it is to respect love.

Just Because

You made my heart whole. You loved it beyond measure. You took what I thought was a disaster and made it your special treasure. When I was face down in the dirt you pulled me out and loved me through all the hurt. When no one cared enough to see about me, you showed up and healed my heart, now it can breathe. You have become my lover, my friend and only if you knew; there's nothing in this world for you I wouldn't do. So to you I dedicate what is now Matters of the Heart. You see it took us a long time to get here and nothing can tear us apart.

I love you for who you are.
I love you for who I now am.
I love you for who we've become.

-Melissa Monék

To my favorite girl. Thank you for always believing in me. Thank you for always supporting me. Thank you for understanding my love and still loving me in spite of. I know you're looking down on me with a smile on your face. Rest well Mama. I Love You!

Roslyn Gail Mackey
October 25, 1955-April 20, 2006

Introduction

Love, you knocked me on my ass; what a hard fall I took. You tore me down so badly, I closed every chapter in my heart's book. Every time I got up you were right there in my face. You haunted and taunted me and here I am thinking you supposed to be a good place. You played with my heart then tore it apart. Regardless of that it loved just as hard. Thanks to you I've learned what type of love I don't want in my life. Thanks to you at the end of my tunnel I see the light.....

Everybody loves at one time or another. No matter for how long, the heart accepts love and the heart gives love. Love allows us to experience joy and happiness. Love also allows the experience of hurt and pain. Love is taken for granted at times. It can also be cherished too much. Love is passion filled. Love is overwhelming. Love needs to be understood and respected. Love touches the heart and makes it flutter in ways never thought of. Love makes the heart and mind do things our mouths say we'll never do. It's funny how love works. But we fall in and out of it every day.

Come journey into my world and experience love the way I see it, understand it, feel it, and respect it. I have experienced love on many different levels. It has taught me, disciplined me, and has allowed me to mature into the woman that I am. Now I share it with you.

-Melissa Monék

To Love Me

To love me is to honor, cherish, trust and believe in me.
To love me is to be open, caring, and understanding.
To love me is to know when I hurt, know when I feel pain, and to know
when I need you.
To love me is to catch me when I fall, be my shoulder to cry on, and to
be a friend to talk to.
To love me is to love me as I love you, to trust me as I trust you,
and to respect me as I respect you.
To love me is to not walk in front of me, to not walk behind me,
but to walk with me as we journey through life together.

My First Love

I once had happiness that I could call my own.
Now just like that, it's all gone.
I once had everything and all that I wanted for.
You brought all of this to me and a whole lot more.
In return, I couldn't give you the happiness that you were seeking.
Now out of my life you are leaving.
When I had you, I thought that what we had was oh so right.
Now alone I lay with many sleepless nights.
I can't think. I can't sleep. I can't live without you.
To have you back into my life, there's nothing I wouldn't do.
You are my everything and my love still grows for you every day.
I wish the wind would blow in my direction so you could come back
my way.
What we shared was very special and will always be to me.
No matter what comes, in my heart you will always be.
Now that you've made your decision and have chosen to move on, I
must put all of this behind. Just know that you'll always live in my heart
and be the first love of mine.

I Came to You

I came to you, a lonely soul, looking for nothing but compassion.
You came to me, full of life, making everything good happen.
I came to you, with a sad heart, not wanting to be hurt.
You came to me, full of happiness, making everything better that could've been worse.
I came to you, seeking love, and also found a best friend.
You came to me, full of love, and allowed me to be happy again.
I came to you, as I am, and you accepted all of that.
You came to me, just the same, and I wanted to give you that acceptance back.
I came to you, not knowing the kind of joy to my life you would bring.
You came to me, not knowing that you walked right out of my dream.
You came to me, and now you're here, and have brightened my life in so many ways.
I came to you, and now I'm here, holding on to Forever-and-Two Days.

A Fool for You

How could I have been so blind to not even see.
How could I have been so blind to not realize that you and I would never be.
How could I have allowed myself to fall for you and give you my best.
How could I not see that when it came to me, you could care less.
How could I have overlooked the fact that your interest were different from mine.
How could I not know that I'd never have you in this lifetime.
How could I have been so naïve to let you play this game and win.
How could you act like I don't mean anything to you when we were more than just friends.
I played the fool for you and now I'm falling apart.
And being such a fool, I believed you when you said you wouldn't break my heart.
The damage is now done and just like that you're gone.
Now this heart of mine, once again, is all alone.

How Could You

How could you say that you love me when all you do is bring me pain.
How could you say that you love me when all the while hurt was your aim.
How could you say that you care about me when to you we don't even matter.
How could you say that you care about me when you're not even trying to make it better.
How could you say that we have forever when we didn't even have a start.
How could you say that we have forever when you're creeping in the dark.
How could you say that this is where you wanna be when unhappy is what you are.
How could you say this is where you wanna be when we're steadily growing apart.
How could you have said any of these things, knowing that you were not ready.
How could you have lead me on, knowing that you never wanted me as your lady.

Love

Love is a word I can't understand.
For some reason it leaves you in a trans.
It gives no answers and asks no questions.
All it does is teaches you lessons.
To fall in love, you need a real strong mind, because to all love is blind.
There is no definition, nor a description.
There is no relationship when love is missing.
To find true love, you need patience and time.
But for me I need a love that's truly mine.
Not a little game or a fairy tale, trying to find love can put you through hell.
Aggravation, disappointments, and also lies,
is what you'll go through for a girl or guy.
Now you think you love someone but it's all in your mind,
because falling in love is like committing a crime.
It happens once, then it happens again, but the third time around you go through pain.
You may get hurt or even upset, letting you know love needs respect.

I Was Wrong

You up and left for a few days only. Without you here, I became very
lonely.
I met a guy who meant me no good. When you returned he was in the
neighborhood.
For talking to him I was wrong, because I knew that you weren't gone
for that long.
But I took the chance and almost lost you. The one I love and whose
heart is true.
I knew you were angry and maybe even upset, because the expressions
on your face I did regret.
It will never happen, never again, because I'm out to win your heart not
bring you pain.
I understand your jealousy because I have it too. Baby, please understand
that I love you.
You may think I'm trying to win you over or sing a sad song. No, it's just
that as your lady, I'm letting you know that I was wrong.

I Gave To You

I gave to you all that a woman could give.
I was pretty sure of you and figured with you I can live.
I gave you an offer no man would have denied.
You took the challenge, being a man, and stripped away my pride.
I gave to you my all, so where did we go wrong.
I thought that we loved each other and had something very strong.
I gave to you a child and also my life.
I took your hand in marriage and became your wife.
I guess that wasn't good enough because of what you did.
If you weren't ready for commitment why keep your feelings hid.
I gave to you the best of me but yet you wanted more.
You said you wanted your freedom and walked out the door.
You walked out of my life and that of your little girls.
You shattered our lives because you were our world.
How could it end this way, after all we've been through.
Just like that you can walk away and start a new life too.
Good luck in your endeavors and whatever you decide to do,
Because you left my heart with hurt and pain after all I gave to you.

Love Lost

Love lost that can't be returned.
Love lost from bridges that have been burned.
Love lost because of pride and dignity.
Love lost because I couldn't face reality.
Love lost and washed away with the rain.
Love lost, leaving hellified pain.
Love lost through the thick and thin, the good and bad.
Love lost to the only love I had.
Love lost, but not yet gone away.
Love lost to be rekindled Forever-and Two Days.

Thoughts of Wonder

I can't help but wonder if we're still important to you.
I can't help but wonder if you still appreciate me too.
I can't help but wonder if your interest in me is leaving.
I can't help but wonder if in us have you stop believing.
I can't help but wonder why you're not into me anymore.
I can't help but wonder if you're ready to walk out the door.
I can't help but wonder if I'll see you any of this day.
I can't help but wonder if we still have Forever-and-Two Days.
I can't help but wonder where your mind is when you're with me.
I can't help but wonder if this is where you really want to be.
I can't help but wonder if I'll ever win your heart.
It hurts me to wonder about what I'd do if we should ever depart.

Here I am

I'm sorry for feeling the way that I do.
But my life has changed since I met you.
You make me feel loved and wanted to be around.
You came into my life and turned my frown upside down.
You made me realize that I could still have happiness.
You stole my heart with a simple kiss.
I'm so into you and don't want to let you go.
But if it has to be that way I'd rather you let me know.
Now that you've got me and we are together,
Can you promise me that we have forever.
You've opened me up to a level of love that's so brand new.
I'm enjoying every minute as long as it's with you.
If you leave me now, I wouldn't know what to do.
Because you've brought me so much joy and I love you.
You may not believe it but yes it's real.
I wasn't sure if I should tell you but you said to speak what I feel.
So here I am giving you my all, accept it or not.
At least I'll know that I've given you all that I've got.

My Feelings For You

You are my brighter days.
You take away the rain.
You came into my life and eased all the pain.
You made me feel loved when no one else cared.
Every time I need you, you're always there.
Thank you for accepting me for me and all that came along with me.
You've shown me that it doesn't matter and that we can really be.
The things you do makes me thankful for the bond that we share.
The things you do makes me realize that you really do care.
How long we will last, neither of us knows.
At least while we're together, let's allow our love to grow.
I appreciate you, I love you, I care for you and so much more.
Baby, you entered my life with open arms and you're the one I adore.
I hope this message gets through to you and you realize how I truly feel.
Because everything I feel for you will always be real.

Crazy Love

My feelings for you are starting to grow.
I want to tell you but my mind says no.
As our friendship has grown, I've become more fond of you.
With the way that I feel, I wish you felt the same way too.
We're two different people, leading two separate lives.
But if at possible, I don't want the chance to pass me by.
I know it may sound silly and I hope you're not offended.
But my feelings for you are more than what I intended.
I don't want to lose our friendship over feeling the way that I do.
But I can't deny my emotions and how much I care about you.
Eventually you'll catch on and understand where I'm coming from.
Hopefully your reaction isn't too bad, then it'll be over and done.
This may be just a phase that I'm going through.
And since I have so much trust, I decided to tell you.
Who may find out now, I don't know.
I just can't keep my feelings hid anymore.
Now that you're at the end I don't know if you'll put our friendship to a
yield.
I just had to tell you about this Crazy Love for you that I feel.

I'm Yours

You said that you hurt and that your heart feels pain.
Let me rescue you so that you can feel love again.
You said that it's been a while since true love has come your way.
Give me time and I'll heal your wounds day by day.
You say that you want me but sometimes I sense you're unsure.
Come into my life and have happiness forever more.
Let me save you from whatever it is that's making you run away.
Let me protect you from it as in my arms you lay.
Believe in me and know that I'll make it right.
I'm ready for you and ready to take you to greater heights.
Let me ease your pain and give you romance.
Take my hand and let me lead you to love's land.
Give me the chance to show you that I'm real.
Let me show you that all that I can do I will.
So put your past behind you and walk through life with me.
I promise you, until death do us part, with you I will always be.

My World

In my world with you is where I always want to be.
But I realize you have a life outside of you and me.
In my world I feel safe from all harm.
I feel so protected when I'm lying in your arms.
In my world with you I have no doubts about anything.
I know that we can conquer any obstacle that this world brings.
In my world with you I feel that nothing can go wrong.
We will always overcome because what we have is strong.
In my world with you no matter what changes may come our way.
In my world with you Forever-and-Two Days.

You and I

You and I are the here and now.
To you and you only I make this vow.
You and I, is it reality or just a dream?
If it's not reality then let me continue to sleep.
You and I are the beginning of our forever.
You and I put the meaning in together.
You and I, no one else, just us two.
Escaping from the world, letting it be all about me and you.
You and I, here we are, both ready and willing.
You and I, both with open hearts, with many mixed feelings.
But yet here we are together as one trying to trust again.
Both afraid of being hurt by love's pain.
So here I am. You got me completely in every way and I'll always be by your side.
No matter what happens, there will always be You and I.

A World Full....

In a world full of hatred, I found true love.
In a world full of noise, I found peace.
In a world full of lies, I found the truth.
In a world full of weakness, I found strength.
In a world full of darkness, I found light.
In a world full of sadness, I found happiness.
In a world full of enemies, I found a friend.
In a world full of wanderers, I found you.

A Part of Me

When I first met you I thought you were just another guy.
One who'd come into my life with all of his white lies.
At first I didn't take you seriously because our relationship was too new.
But as time passed on my love for you grew.
It grew to the point where a part of me left my soul.
A part of me which went to you, a part I hope you can hold.
A part of me which I hated to take away from myself.
But when a love is as true as yours, I'd rather share it with no one else.
You made me feel how much you really care.
That's why with you a part of me was shared.
Now that it's being shared, I hope you don't take it for granted.
Because inside my heart you have truly implanted.
Implanted your love which I don't want to lose.
But you must realize receiving a part of me is not to be abused.
You were the one who finally came along.
Without many fantasies or sad little songs.
Therefore, I let a part of me leave.
A part of me that I do not want to retrieve.
So keep your love strong as long as we are meant to be.
Because you have truly earned a Part of Me.

Suddenly

Suddenly I'm having these feelings that I thought would never surface
again.
Suddenly I found someone who's become my lover and my best friend.
Suddenly I find myself day dreaming about you all day.
Suddenly I'm finding myself wanting to be with you in every way.
Suddenly my heart is opening up once more.
Suddenly it feels real love knocking at its door.
Suddenly my fears are beginning to disappear.
Suddenly into my life you are here.
Suddenly my life has new meaning.
Suddenly I realized that I'm not dreaming.
Suddenly we are together, two strangers becoming the best of friends.
Suddenly I want you forever until the end.
I found someone with a real sense of trust for me.
Now I'm ready to fall in love, Suddenly.

Let Me Love You

Baby let me love you from your head to your feet.
All of your sexual desires, undoubtedly, I will meet.
Baby let me love you from your wildest dream to your wildest fantasy.
Let me take you to the highest level of ecstasy.
Baby let me love you in all the right places.
Oh it's gonna be a homerun, 'cause I'll cover all the bases.
Baby let me love you and moan when I hit the right spots.
I bet I'll have you screaming and it won't be because you want to stop.
Baby let me love you so gentle and divine.
'cause once these hands touch you you'll go into a relaxed state of mind.
Baby let me love you erasing all of your stress from this day.
Let me love you 'til it feels better and believe me I have so many ways.
Baby let me love you. I'm better than any drug.
I can't be prescribed by any doctor or sold by any thug.
Finally, baby let me love you taking you through excitements every
phase.
But more importantly let me love you Forever-and Two Days.

Hand in Hand

Hand in hand from different walks of life we come.
Hand in hand we have become one.
Hand in hand we've vowed to be together.
Hand in hand we vowed to love forever.
Hand in hand you've won my heart.
Hand in hand so we'll never depart.
Hand in hand from the very first day.
Hand in hand I knew I'd have you always.
Hand in hand from beginning to end.
Hand in hand you've become my lover and my best friend.
Hand in hand, side by side we will forever be.
Hand in hand I belong to you and you belong to me.
Hand in hand through the thick and thin.
Hand in hand with the strength of our love we will always win.
Hand in hand is what we are n more than one way.
Hand in hand Forever-and-Two Days.

Whose Is It

He was my man and you were just a fling.
We saw each other secretly not knowing the trouble it would bring.
I was in love with him but played around with you.
I slept with him and I slept with you too.
The times we were together were times well spent.
And all the while he had no hints.
I tried to be true to him to keep his trust.
But being with you became a must.
I couldn't leave him and I didn't want to let you go.
So I kept our affair on the down low.
A few months later I was carrying someone's baby.
Whose is it, I don't know and now I'm going crazy.
Neither of you know but yet it is true.
I am carrying a child and I don't know from who.
Maybe I could get rid of it before either of you find out.
I thought it would work but still had my doubts.
Whose is it or who shall I say is the father?
Should I tell my man about you or should I even bother?
Whose is it and what shall I do?
To not break up my happy home I'm gonna go on with my life and try
to forget about you.

Thinking of You

Every time I close my eyes you come into my mind.
Who would have thought that this kind of happiness I would find.
You brighten up my days with all of your joy and laughter.
Who would have thought that my heart you would capture.
My whole life has become centered around you.
You make me so happy with everything that you do.
When I think about you joy comes over me.
When I think about you with you is where I wanna be.
You have given me a reason to wanna love again.
You came into my life and erased all my pain.
With you I am secure. With you I feel safe.
You have become a part of me and in my heart you have a special place.
I have everything in the world to offer you but only so much can I give.
All I know is that with you I want to live.
This is just a little something to let you know you're on my mind.
I'm telling you now and will tell you often because with you true love I
did find.

How Do You

How do you say I'm sorry when you've caused someone so much pain?
How do you stop the tears from falling like the rain?
How do you say I love you to someone who's completely captured your heart?
How do you keep them around when they want to depart?
How do you get someone to realize how much you really do care?
How do you begin to start when you have so much to share?
How do you say to someone give our love another chance when their mind is made up?
How do you try to convince them when you're third strike you've struck?
How do you get someone to understand how you really feel?
How do you get them to see that your love for them is real?
How do you get someone to see any of this when they don't want to?
If it's worth the fight give it your all but to yourself remain true.

Lonely Heart

Happiness once lived here and a smile stayed on my face.
Now this broken heart of mine has become a lonely place.
It used to be a place that was filled with joy and laughter.
It used to be a place that wished for happily ever after.
Now it's a place that has grown very cold and dark,
because it has surrendered to so many broken hearts.
It once had a reason to love and allowed me to give the best of me.
It once had compassion, allowing me to overlook the wrong in you that
others did see.
There was a time when this heart would give all that it had.
Now it's just a lonely place with memories that are sad.
But no more will this heart be lonely because love will always be there.
And it knows that somewhere, with another, love it can share.

I'm Not Gonna Cry

I'm not gonna cry when I find numbers in your pants pockets.
I'm not gonna cry when you look me in the face and lie about it.
I'm not gonna cry when the phone calls start coming.
I'm not gonna cry when it's me you stop loving.
I'm not gonna cry when I see you holding her hand.
I'm not gonna cry because I know I'm a better woman.
I'm not gonna cry when the walls come tumbling down.
I'm not gonna cry not even if you don't come back around.
I'm not gonna cry when the truth finally comes out.
I'm not gonna cry, not even scream or shout.
I'm not gonna cry when you finally walk out of that door.
I'm not gonna cry because you cannot hurt me anymore.

Love's Hurt

I feel the pain that love constantly brings to me.
I feel the pain once again of being lonely.
I feel the pain that love has brought back into my heart.
I feel the pain of us now being apart.
I feel the pain that love has me drowning in.
I feel the pain from the thought of you only wanting a friend.
I feel the pain that keeps shattering my heart into pieces.
Yet, it continues to love for so many unknown reasons.
I feel the pain and burden that love has put back on me.
It hurts like hell knowing happiness I'll never see.
I feel the pain and it's not a good feeling at all.
Love has hurt me again because I've allowed myself to fall.
I've fallen for you and like everyone else, you made me experience
Love's hurt because you looked out for self.

Fantasy

I went to our favorite place today hoping to find you there.
I looked high and low but couldn't find you anywhere.
As I began to leave I heard your voice whisper my name.
It was so sweet and soft but when I looked from nowhere you came.
I thought my mind was playing tricks on me when you I thought I
did see.
You're over one hundred miles away so I know our favorite place you
couldn't be.
I said to myself, "You've got to get it together".
Then I realized you were gone but not gone forever.
So as I walked down the path I stopped at the pond.
And when I looked in I saw a reflection of you holding me in your arms.
At that time I received a tap on my shoulder and what a sight to see.
I became filled with joy because you were really there with me.
I pinched myself to make sure I wasn't dreaming and said what a dream
come true.
But all of it was just a fantasy because of how much I'm missing you.

Say That

Say that you will love me forever and will never leave my side.
Say that you will love me forever and that you'll always be mine.
Say that you will care for me when I need you most of all.
Say that you will care for me enough to catch me when I fall.
Say that you will always need me and forever feel the need to want me.
Say that you will need me enough to make home where you want to be.
Say that I have you completely in every single way.
Honestly say that I have you Forever-and-Two Days.
Say that I can confide in you all of my inner thoughts.
Say that I can confide in you because my trust you've already got.
Say that you will always be here and you'll never break my heart.
Say that you will always be here until death does us apart.

In Friendship and In Love

In friendship and in love I'll always cherish the bond that we share.
Because you've shown me with compassion that you really do care.
You have shown me a lot of things and have taught me quite a bit.
That's why you're the one I'm in love with.
Although we've had our quarrels and our share of ups and downs,
You were always there for me and able to get a smile from a frown.
Whenever I need you, you always answer my call.
You've shown me that you love me and that you'd never let me fall.
In friendship and in love we've overcome great obstacles,
proving to the world that a love like ours is possible.
In friendship and in love with you I will always share my heart.
I'll always stand by your side no matter who or what tries to tear us
apart.

Assurance

Baby, assure me that you won't break my heart.
Assure me that we will never depart.
You're all I've got and my world revolves around you.
If you were to leave me I wouldn't know what to do.
There'd be no reason for loving again, let alone living.
Because to you my all I have given.
I want to hold you tight and never let you slip away.
I'm gonna enjoy it while it last because eventually you will one day.
We've been through too much and what we have is too strong.
So baby, don't give up, hold on.
You say that you love me, care for me, and the whole nine.
But what I need to know is, are you completely mine?
I love you, I care for you, and there's nothing in this world for you I
wouldn't do.
All I need you to be is patient and understanding and know that it's all
about you.

The Way of Love

Love, that BIG little word.
Some say it's good others say it's grand.
But I think it's nothing but hurt and pain.
The lies to go through and all of the games,
with no one in the world to choose to blame.
You think about it once and think it's the pits.
Then you realize that you want to call it quits.
Don't let love take over you because if you do,
Love is the one thing that will make a fool out of you.
You'll say you hate him or that you hate her,
taking you back to when you met each other.
Yeah, it was love at first sight.
But you were blind to the fact that there would be fusses and fights.
Fights that you thought would never occur.
The ones that took you back to the people you were.
The people you were before you met on another,
when you both were friends, not thinking of being lovers.
But after you started dating it became a different story.
Now with this relationship all you do is worry.
You're afraid of losing her and she's afraid of losing you,
when you both claim to have a love that is true.
So to settle your problems listen to me.

This is the way that it should be.
When the night is young and the sky is new,
just hold each other close and whisper
I Love You!

A Variety of Love

A love so deep, a love so rare.
A love with you I only want to share.
A love so open, a love so new.
A love that I can finally share with you.
A love so unique, a love so divine.
A love that I can call all mine.
A love that wraps me softly in its arms.
A love that won me over with its charm.
A love so kind, a love so gentle.
A love not only physical but also mental.
A love unconditional, a love so defined.
A love that gives me peace at mind.
A love that is yours, a love that is mine.
A love we'll share until the end of time.

Are You The One

Sometimes I wonder if I'm playing against the odds.
Sometimes I wonder if I laid out too many cards.
Sometimes I wonder if this will ever be.
Sometimes I wonder are you the one for me.
Sometimes I sit here waiting all day just to hear from you.
Sometimes I wonder if I'm playing the fool.
Sometimes I sense that you want me. Sometimes I sense that you care.
But when we're together your mind seems to be elsewhere.
I'm trying my best to do what's right.
But it seems like I'm in a no win fight.
I can't keep opening up if you keep rejecting me time after time.
I can't keep trying if you don't want to be mine.
I can only do what I can, hoping you'll meet me halfway.
And if it's meant to be, I know you'll be mine one day.
So please don't let me down. Please prove me wrong.
Know that it will work if we both stand strong.

Today I Realized

Today I realized the beginning of my end.
Today I realized I need you to be more than just my friend.
Today I realized the beginning of a better way.
Today I realized I'm ready for us each and every day.
Today I realized that I'm a stronger person because of all we've been through.
Today I realized that I don't want to live my life without you.
Today I realized that you're the only one for me.
Today I realized for you a better person I want to be.
Today I realized I want to put the past completely behind.
Today I realized I'm gonna make you mine.
Today I realized that we're two different people who chose to become one.
Today I realized that we'll still be together when it's all said and done.
Today I realized that I'm gonna give you the best that I've got.
I'm gonna give it to you whether you want it or not.
Understand that I'm not perfect but I'm gonna give you my all.
This time around I'm not gonna let us fall.

From Me To You

When I was being difficult you were very understanding.
When I was sad you brought me joy.
When I cried you wiped away my tears.
When I was happy you were there to share my laughter.
Because of these little things that you do
My love has grown for you in a very special way.
You have become a very special part of my life.
A part that I hope never goes away.
You are my comforter, my friend, and a good lover.
Being with you is the best thing that could have ever happened to me.
Thank you for making my life complete.
Thank you for accepting me.
Thank you for putting up with me.
Thank you for understanding me.
But most of all thank you for loving me the beautiful way that you are.
I Love You.

Twelve Twenty-Three

For so many years I've known you to be a great man.
No matter what, I knew our love would always withstand.
The passion and love we share is like none other.
You have truly answered all of my thoughts of wonder.
The miles we've walked and the journeys we've taken
have brought us to a place that was by no means mistaken.
On that special day we opened our hearts and let them speak
and the outcome of that is our Twelve Twenty-Three.
I placed my heart in your hands at that very moment and fell in love so
deep.
Now each and every day I thank you for allowing Us to become a We.
You make my heart smile time after time
because baby you are my Sunshine.
You are truly the reason for everything good that I now do see.
You are that reason thanks to our Twelve Twenty-Three.
My heart skips a beat to know that I am the Air You Breathe.
My heart melts over and over to know that you are in love with me.
Now that we're here I don't want us to let it go
because no matter what lies ahead this is just the beginning of our road.
Know that I'm here; you've got me for as long as we can be.
No matter what happens nothing can erase our Twelve Twenty-Three.

Love Me When It Hurts

It took a long time to get to where we are.
It's good to know that we can share our love from afar.
Just the thought of how good your love feels to me,
takes me to a whole new level of ecstasy.
I mean, your love is so great; it knocks me off of my feet.
You let me know that I'm number one and for you I don't have to
compete.
It's all good, knowing that you will always keep me first.
But baby what I need, is for you to love me when it hurts.
When I need it the most, I need to know that you'll be there.
When I reach out to you,
I need to know that you really do care.
When it hurts like hell and the pain is so real,
that's when the love you have for me, I need to feel.
You've shown me that you can love me in the good times,
but will you love me in the bad;
when my heart is crying out to you because it's lonely and sad.
Hold me, comfort me, and take me in your arms.
Let my heart know you'll protect it from all harm.
Because loving you is one of the best things that I can do on this earth,
it makes my heart smile to know that you love me, especially when it
hurts.

My Lover, My Friend

My lover, my friend how can I ask for more.
You made my life complete when you came knocking at my heart's door.
My lover, my friend, can't everyone say they have that in their world.
I can so proudly say it because you made me your girl.
My lover, my friend holding back nothing at all.
Because of the love that we share, I promise to never let us fall.
My lover and a good lover you are indeed.
My friend and the best one whenever I'm in need.
My friend who became my lover or my lover who became my friend.
No matter how you look at it, we have us until time ends.
My lover, my friend wow, I never thought this would be.
But you proved me wrong on that special day, our twelve twenty-three.
So to you I promise to be the best friend ever and even a greater lover.
I promise every time I touch you, I will make your heart flutter.
My lover, my friend what more can I say.
We compliment each other in every single way.
I'm the left and you're the right.
You're the up and I'm the down.
It's so amazing how we built our foundation on such solid ground.
Nothing can come between us, no matter who or what may try;
because this kind of love and friendship is not one that you can buy.
So know that what we share could never be pretend;
because you have truly proven to be my lover, my friend.

Matters Of The Heart

Matters of the heart, that of mine and yours.
Matters of the heart because they were knocking at each other's door.
If the heart doesn't matter then the love won't exist;
because without matters of the heart, it's just hers and his.
No us, no we, not even an our;
when it's not understood that matters of the heart has great power.
Not your half, not my half, but our whole together.
When we put matters of the heart first, we'll always have forever.
I love you with all that matters in my heart because your heart is all that
matters to me.
You see you're holding my heart and there's no other place I'd rather
it be.
Because you understand that matters of the heart is a very fragile issue,
I know there can't be a better place than my heart being with you.
Matters of the heart, you say how can that really be.
Understand that when it comes to love, the heart feels what the eyes
can't see.
It feels the love, it feels the passion, it feels the hurt, and it feels the pain.
Matters of the heart is what allows us to love over and over again.
No matter what you go through, no matter how many times,
it doesn't even matter how far you two are apart;
if you've got a love that's strong,
it will always last because of matters of the heart.

Once In a Lifetime

Once in a lifetime that special someone will come your way.
Know how to see past the hurt and pain to make that one stay.
Once in a lifetime you're gonna get that love that's real.
Know how to get past your old heartbreaks, and this one allow your heart to feel.
Once in a lifetime you're gonna get that happiness you thought you didn't deserve.
Now that you have it know how to come out of reserve.
Don't allow your heart to miss out on its once and lifetime;
because no matter what it's been through, it knows what it feels like to say this is all mine.
That once in lifetime is so unique and so very rare.
Open up your heart because love with you it wants to share.
Don't run away from it, reject it, or even put it on hold;
because that once in a lifetime wants to love that heart of yours, the one that's so cold.
You've put it up forever, for whatever the reasons may be;
but that once in a lifetime is here to show you that it can once again be happy.
Understand that once in a lifetime is just that.
Don't let it pass you by because you may never be able to get it back.
I found my once in a lifetime and I found it in you.
I promise to hold on tight and let you do what it is that you do.

So I say to you, thank you for coming into this dark world of mine,
with no holds barred, and letting your sun shine.
Thank you for seeing pass all my hurt and pain,
becoming my once in a lifetime.

If Loving You Is Wrong

If loving you is wrong, I will never know right;
because everything seems so real when I lay you down at night.
If loving you is wrong, I'm guilty so charge me with life;
because everything I feel for you, it feels so real, it can't be a lie.
If loving you is wrong, then wrong must be the new right;
because baby loving you takes me to greater heights.
If loving you is wrong, please don't correct me.
You see the love I have for you, it will never cease.
So I'd rather be wrong if it means my love for you don't have to end.
But if that's not the case I'd rather be wrong time and time again.

The Air You Breathe

When you feel that good sensation, you know, the one that makes you
smile.
Know that it's the air you breathe; you can feel it for miles and miles.
When you feel like you can't go on and oxygen is what you need.
Just inhale real big and you'll have the air you breathe.
You will never have to worry about running out of a supply of air;
because the air you breathe will always be there.
You may not be able to see it but trust me it will always keep you
revived.
Baby the air you breathe is what's keeping your heart alive.
Alive in the sense of happy and keeping it with a smile.
Alive in the sense that it will never have a frown.
The air you breathe, baby, it's for a lifetime;
because the love that we share is so rare, so defined.
Don't you ever worry about being short of breath
because the air you breathe will always be good for your health.
Inhale it, breathe it, and take it all in;
because baby with this air that you breathe our love can never end.

You Are My Sunshine

You came into my life shining so freely and so bright.
You came into my life turning my darkness to light.
You came into my life so radiantly but oh so calm.
You came into my life letting me know that the sun does shine after the
storm.
You are my sunshine. You shine so brightly in my life giving me a brand
new glow.
Your rays are so powerful through me, they can't help but show.
It gives me a good feeling because your warmth just soothes my soul.
Because you are my sunshine, you led me off that dark and lonely road.
You brought my heart back to life, giving it a reason to love again.
You came into my life being that sunshine after the rain.
No matter how torn, no matter how broken, no matter how low I felt
face down in the dirt.
You became my light at the end of the tunnel because you loved me
through all the hurt.
You are my sunshine. You sit so high I wanna place you on a throne.
A throne in my heart because that's now your new home.
I thank you for choosing me. I thank you for accepting me.
I thank you for allowing your heart to open up and love mine.
Baby I thank you, for you are my sunshine.

If Only You Knew

If only you knew how my heart skips a beat every time you come around.
If only you knew how you've turned my heart's frown upside down.
If only you knew of the happiness you've brought back to me.
If only you knew that you've made my life a better place to be.
If only you knew that you have become my world.
If only you knew all of this happened when you made me your girl.
If only you knew how much you are healing my heart.
If only you knew I love who I'm becoming because of who we are.
If only you knew I can now see in color.
If only you knew my life's on a new path and I'd rather share it with none other.
If only you knew the sensation I feel from your touch.
If only you knew how I long for you so much.
If only you knew I can't see my life without you or your life without me.
If only you knew how I don't mind being held in your captivity.
If only you knew I fell in love with you so hard and so deep.
If only you knew with you is the only place I wanna be.
If only you knew at my weakest point you made me so strong.
If only you knew in my heart, you're now that new song.
If only you knew that with our love your ego can be conceited.
If only you knew that you're the best thing I never knew I needed.
You're so good for me and in return I'm so good for you.
I love you with all my heart, body, and spirit.
Baby if only you knew.

Love Without You

Love without you, that I cannot imagine.
Love without you would be like feelings without passion.
Love without you, I can't keep that thought boxed in;
because love without you would be like life without oxygen.
Love without you, my mind won't even go that far;
because love without you would be like the ending with no start.
I've had the pleasure of loving you so I don't see love without you.
If you took that away from me I really wouldn't know what to do.
I would probably go crazy or maybe lose my mind;
because baby love without you would be like the sun with no shine.

My Last First Kiss

Is there such a thing as having a last first kiss?
Well I had mine, that very day when you held my hand and gently
kissed my lips.
You are my last first kiss, that I would've never thought of;
because with everything I already felt for you,
it was our first kiss that with you, I instantly fell in love.
You are my last first kiss no matter how many more we have.
Because that first kiss I had with you my soul it did grab.
It wrapped me up so tightly and made sure I didn't fall.
My last first kiss had me walking before I crawled.
Before I knew it you were holding my heart in your hands.
I didn't even want it back because I was loving the job description and
the benefit plan.
My last first kiss, that's who you are even though I didn't know it was a
such thing.
My last first kiss keeps my heart with a new song to sing.
The songs are never out of tune and they never seem to get old.
They keep my heart smiling and warms my soul.
My last first kiss will be that kiss I'll always remember,
from that cold winter night when you held me in December.
All my dreams came true that very night,
from when upon a star I did wish.
Now I have you in my life and you are my last first kiss.

Come Into My Life

Come into my life and let me give you all that I can.
Come into my life and experience real romance.
Come into my life and share with me forever.
Come into my life and promise you'll leave me never.
Come into my life and be together with me.
Come into my life and only happiness you will see.
Come into my life so as one we can finally be.
Come into my life so I can satisfy all of your needs.
Come into my life ready, willing, and able.
Come into my life wanting a relationship with a foundation that's stable.
Come into my life but leave your fantasy world behind.
Come into my life and everything you're searching for you will find.
I want to enter your world and see how you're living.
Then, I'll bring you to mine and give you everything you're missing.
My world is filled with so much love, joy, and laughter.
Baby when you come into my life you won't have to worry a day after.
So come into my life if you're ready to experience your life's new plan.
But also, come into my life by choice not by chance.

Crazy Love The Sequel

Here I am once again, confronting this crazy love that I have.
The only difference this time is that it's on a better path.
I opened up to you on paper oh so long ago;
not knowing all these years later I would have the courage to let you know.
I poured out my heart to you sharing all about you that's meaningful.
Your heart gladly accepted and now we have crazy love, the sequel.
The way our hearts opened up and talked to one another,
surprised the hell out of me because it couldn't have chosen a better lover.
That crazy love that I held so deep within,
finally came out, and now you're my lover, my friend.
Crazy love, yeah baby that's all it was back then;
because no matter what I felt, I knew we couldn't be no more than just friends.
But when the truth came out and I laid out all my cards to be seen;
your heart gladly accepted, letting me know this wasn't just a dream.
So now here we are becoming one and sharing all of our dreams together.
Whether it's crazy love or crazy love the sequel,
just know that we have it forever.

Love of My Life

Come and lay with me, let me ease your mind.
Let me kiss you; let me hold you till the end of time.
Forget about you pass 'cause it's a new day.
I'm here to make you happy in every single way.
I know all your hurt. I know all your pain;
but baby, I'm that sunshine after the rain.
So have no worries, have no fears
because real love for your heart is finally here.
Close your eyes and let me be your guide.
Hold on tight and enjoy the ride.
I'll never let you down on this you can bet.
Believe me baby you ain't seen nothing yet.
There ain't no other, I'm one of a kind.
I'll be here for you at the drop of a dime.
Your wish is my command, my every desire.
Baby you're the one who lights my heart on fire.
From the moment that I saw you, I knew you'd be mine.
You came into my life and you let your light shine.
Now my world is yours, it revolves around you.
And there's nothing in this world for you I wouldn't do.
So baby take my hand and come with me.
Let me take you to tha t level of ecstasy.
This is not a front; no it's not a game.

Our love means more to me than any riches or fame.
I stay on cloud nine 'cause you keep so high.
You're better than any drug, I ain't gonna lie.
Let me wrap myself around you and hold you close
'cause your love to me is like an overdose.
Twenty-four seven I'm thinking of you.
Where you at, what you're doing and baby with who?
I'll protect from this world in my safe place.
Baby you don't have to worry, I won't go astray.
I'm here today, tomorrow, and forever.
I'm here for you and I'm down for whatever.

Looking For Love

Looking for love but didn't know where to start.
Looking for love that's coming straight from the heart.
Looking for love but searched all the wrong places.
Looking for love to fill these empty spaces.
Looking for love and a fool for it too.
Looking for love that's going to be true.
Looking for love that I've yet to find.
Looking for love that's going to be mine.
Looking for love but finding hurt and pain.
Looking for love with the chance of my heart being broken over and
over again.
I was looking for love but too blind to see
that the love I thought I was finding was not the love for me.
Looking for that one love who'd be there when I fall.
The one who'd be there to love me through it all.
Looking for love but ready to let the search go,
not knowing that love was on the other side of the door.
Looking for love and I finally found it in you.
You came into my life and made my heart feel brand new.
So with all the hurt and pain I've allowed my heart to endure,
I thank you for rescuing it and giving it a cure.
Looking for love and now I know it was well worth the wait.

You made it well worth it when you healed my heart from past heartaches.
When I think about us I realize that you must have been sent from heaven up above.
You were sent into my life so I no longer have to look for love.

Look Into My Eyes

Look into my eyes and tell me what you see.
A product of disaster, naw, that's no longer me.
I got my act together, now I'm rising to shine.
Before it's all over "The World Will Be Mine."
I've become so focused, man I'm chasing my dreams.
I'm putting the past behind me; it's time to come clean.
As these thoughts race through my mind, they're driving me wild.
They say I wouldn't make it but I'm on my last mile.
I got a one track mind and I won't be stopped.
No matter how hard you try, I'm gonna make it to the top.
I'm going full blast. I feel it in my veins.
This time around, it's not from life's pain.
My childhood gone. Nothing of it left to share,
but the pain and the memories of why I was there.
My mind started wandering and I stopped dreaming.
There was nothing in this world again that I could believe in.
So I got tatted up at a very young age.
Thought it would take away the pain but it only built rage.
Rage that I had for everyone who didn't care.
Rage that I had because no one was there.
Then it happened all at once. I remember that night.
It all flashed before me right before I took my life.

But God stepped in and quickly changed the plan.
He made it all better when he took me by the hand.
You see, a product of a disaster, I will no longer ever be.
Now, look into my eyes and tell me what you see.

You Can't Hurt Me Anymore

You took away my innocence like a thief in the night.
Then you tried to comfort it like everything was alright.
You led me to believe that what you were doing to me was okay.
I can't believe I suffered through the pain day after day.
You violated my body time after time.
Said you wasn't worried because if anyone found out, it would be your
word against mine.
How can I fight this, I didn't know what to do.
While all the while I was being used and abused.
Why didn't I do anything. Why didn't I say anything. Why didn't I tell.
At that age I didn't have the courage so my life became a living hell.
Because of you I lost trust in men and that wasn't hard to do.
You see you left me so torn my heart continued to accept love's abuse.
For so long you had me trapped in my past still living through the hurt.
I finally got strong enough and built up my nerve.
I built them up enough to tell myself you can't hurt me anymore.
It was now time to sweep all the hurt out the door.
My pain stayed captive for so very long.
But now I got the strength to say pain be gone.
You can't hurt me, no not anymore.
Because I'm not that weak child you took advantage of sometime before.

So know that you can no longer ever hurt me again.
I refuse to let that be.
Because I've taken what you've done
and instead of being a victim I'm becoming a better me.

You Don't Have To Love Me

You don't have to love me because I've learned to love myself.
You don't have to love me even after I've become a stranger to everyone
else.
You don't have to love me no, not any more.
You took that along with you when you walked out the door.
You don't have to love me because your kind of love I don't need.
You don't have to love me because your kind of love makes my heart
bleed.
You don't have to love me especially if you don't want to.
And I sure as hell don't want you to love me if your love is not true.
You don't have to love me because my love comes from within.
You see you don't have to love me because my heart will always mend.
So you can take your love and do with it whatever it is you please.
Because believe me, your kind of love my heart doesn't need.

Trust

I give you my heart entrusting my life to you.
You've become my world just by the simple things you do.
Now that you hold my life in the palm of your hands;
I'm loving the way you love me, like no one else can.
I give you my all, my everything, my best;
because you came and fixed my broken heart when it was a train wreck.
I give you my trust because baby you've earned that and more.
At my weakest point, you came into my life and everything in it you
restored.
I trust your mind, I trust your heart, I trust the words you say.
I trust you so much that I fall in love with you over and over every day.
You came to me looking for nothing but to gain the love in my heart.
What I didn't know was that you'd paint it with so many beautiful
colors, like priceless art.
You've painted a new picture and I love the way it looks.
Baby this feels so good I know it can't be found in any books.
You came so passionate, and looking for nothing in return you came so
real.
You came to me loving me so hard making
sure that joy and happiness was all that my heart did feel.
Thank you for coming into this broken life of mine and taking my heart
out of reserve.
So take a stand, take a bow my love because my trust you deserve.

Giving Myself To You

I never thought I'd give myself freely to anyone else.
I never thought that with you I could just be myself.
You came into my life and made it a wonderful place to be.
That's why it's so easy giving you all of me.
I never thought this kind of happiness would ever find me again.
But baby you've come into my life, allowing my heart to finally win.
I can stand before you with my flaws and all.
I can freely give you my heart knowing you won't let me fall.
Giving myself to you, baby you have made that so easy to do.
I give you my mind, body, spirit and my whole heart too.
You have allowed me to experience a love that I never thought would
come true.
I thank you for that as I give myself to you.
You keep my heart full of joy and you keep a smile on my face.
The love that you give me keeps me in such a great place.
So as I stand here before you amazed with all of the simple things
you do.
I give you my all in all and I'm giving myself to you.

In The Morning

I've fallen in love so deeply and I'm giving myself to you.
When this evening ends will you be here with the morning's dew.
I've opened up so much and put my heart in your hands.
Now that I have, in the morning, will I still be a part of your plans.
I know we will have our ups and downs and maybe even our fuss and
fights.
But what I need to know, is will you be here when the sun rise.
When the storm ends and we've made it through the night,
can you promise me you'll still be here by my side.
I don't expect for us to be perfect but yet I want us to be so very close.
You see baby our love is off the Richter scale, we have no status quo.
In the morning will I be able to look into your eyes and see that you're
still next to me.
Will I be able to hold you and feel you, knowing that this is where you
wanna be.
Don't take my love for granted because you have it all not just some.
I will always be here by your side when the morning comes.
Just accept it, nurture it, protect it, and appreciate everything from it
we're becoming.
Because when the dust clears and the night ends we'll always have in the
morning.

Rest Of My Life

For the rest of my life, I vow to give you my all.
I promise to always protect you and never let us fall.
For the rest of my life, I will be everything that you want and need.
I promise that all of your expectations, I will exceed.
For the rest of my life, you will be the only love I know.
I promise to nurture, protect, and allow our love to grow.
For the rest of my life, you will hold my heart in your hands.
I promise to love you like no one else can.
For the rest of my life, to keep you happy, I will do whatever it takes.
I promise to be your perfect soul mate.
No matter when, where, or how, girl this to you I vow.
My life, my love, my spirit, my heart
because baby you had it all right from the start.
You came into my life making all of my dark places so very bright.
You loved me so hard and through all the hurt,
so to you I give the rest of my life.

All Cried Out

When we met you brought so much joy into my life.
From the beginning, I knew one day you'd make me your wife.
You had so much to offer and so many promises to give.
Like a fool, I fell for you and for you only I lived.
I abandoned myself from society and became a stranger to the world.
I centered my life around you while you cheated with other girls.
I over looked your wrong because of love and was too blind to see.
So I forgave you as usual and let you come back to me.
Now I'm all cried out and I have no more tears to cry.
I can no longer go on like this, I can't keep believing your lies.
You've hurt me enough, now I've gotta move on.
And before you get another chance, I'd rather be alone.
I'm all cried out from all of your hurt and pain.
Because of you, I have to start all over again.
Nevertheless, with this new life that I start, it will surrender to no more
broken hearts.
So I say to you thank you for showing me the kind of love that you're
about.
I'm packing up and moving on because my heart is all cried out.

Our Special Place

I see the beauty. I feel the peace. I feel the freedom and I wanna stay.
This is what I see when I close my eyes and vision our special place.
It's a place of warmth. It's a place where our love can grow.
It's a place where no one has traveled and no other hearts can go.
It's our special place, made for only you and I.
Baby this is one place with me you don't ever have to be shy.
We're free to be who we are, there's no boundaries or limits.
It's our special place so we make all the rules in it.
Our special place, oh how I love to go there.
When the moon glistens on the sand, what a beautiful glare.
It's a place that's so perfect, a place filled with so much calm.
In our special place we can weather any storm.
Our special place, yes it's just yours and mine.
Our special place, a place we can go at any given time.
Baby let me take you there each and every day.
In our special place you can always have your way.
Relax your mind and let your body be free.
Because in our special place it's all about you and me.
No outsiders, no intruders, no interruptions.
Just good love making with plenty of exotic eruptions.
So baby no matter what obstacles during your day you may face;
just know that I'm waiting to relieve all that stress in our special place.

Saving Forever

I'm saving forever because you're that love that I've been looking for.
I'm saving forever because you're that love I found and so much more.
I'm saving forever because I have a lifetime with you.
You are the reason I now do the things that I do.
You keep my spirit glowing. You keep my heart with a smile.
That's why I'm saving forever, 'cause I don't want it for just a little while.
Baby, I'm saving forever, so you got me for more than just a lifetime.
For as long as you want me and need me, I'm here until the end of time.
I almost gave up on love after being in it a time or two.
But now that there's an us, I'm saving forever for you.
You gave me new hope on this thing called love.
You must be an angel sent from heaven up above.
The way you embrace me, the way you accept me, and the way you
make me feel;
I know that a love like ours has got to be real.
That's why I'm saving forever because I'm looking forward to our road
ahead.
You see, our love is like that best seller the one that everyone's read.
So hold on tight baby as we make it through all the stormy weather.
And know that no matter what, for you, I'm saving forever.

About the Book

A book of love on every level. This book is combined with poetry for every heart. It helps you understand the depths of love and the things we endure trying to find it. A must read for the heart that needs to know that love doesn't always have to hurt. Love can find you when you least expect it. Let M.O.T.H. take you on that journey.